High Technology
Drones
by Julie Murray
Dash!
LEVELED READERS
3
An Imprint of Abdo Zoom • abdobooks.com

**Level 1 – Beginning**
Short and simple sentences with familiar words or patterns for children who are beginning to understand how letters and sounds go together.

**Level 2 – Emerging**
Longer words and sentences with more complex language patterns for readers who are practicing common words and letter sounds.

**Level 3 – Transitional**
More developed language and vocabulary for readers who are becoming more independent.

**abdobooks.com**

Published by Abdo Zoom, a division of ABDO, PO Box 398166, Minneapolis, Minnesota 55439.


Printed in the United States of America, North Mankato, Minnesota.
052020
092020

Photo Credits: Alamy, Getty Images, Granger Collection, iStock, Shutterstock, US Navy
Production Contributors: Kenny Abdo, Jennie Forsberg, Grace Hansen, John Hansen
Design Contributors: Dorothy Toth, Neil Klinepier, Laura Graphenteen

**Library of Congress Control Number: 2019956152**

**Publisher's Cataloging in Publication Data**

Names: Murray, Julie, author.
Title: Drones / by Julie Murray
Description: Minneapolis, Minnesota : Abdo Zoom, 2021 | Series: High technology | Includes online resources and index.
Identifiers: ISBN 9781098221164 (lib. bdg.) | ISBN 9781098222147 (ebook) | ISBN 9781098222635 (Read-to-Me ebook)
Subjects: LCSH: Drone aircraft--Juvenile literature. | Vehicles, Remotely piloted--Juvenile literature. | Robotics--Juvenile literature. | High technology--Juvenile literature. | Technological innovations--Juvenile literature.
Classification: DDC 629.892--dc23

# Table of Contents

# Drones

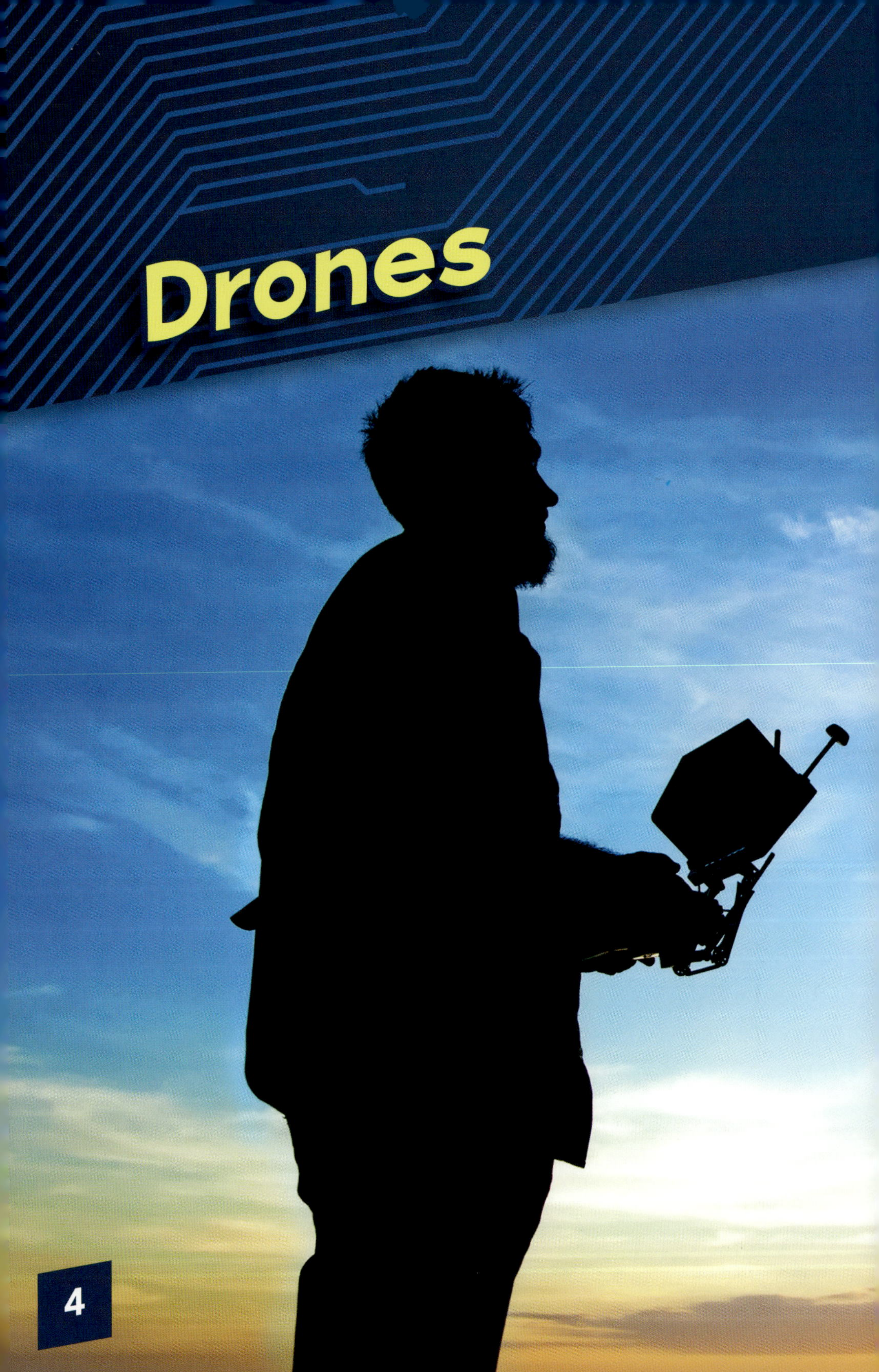

A drone is a flying machine. It is an unmanned aerial vehicle (UAV). This means it has no pilot on board. Some drones are flown by pilots on the ground. The pilots use remote controls. Others use **computers** to fly on their own.

UAVs have been around for a long time. The first of its kind was used in 1849. Austrian soldiers attacked the city of Venice, Italy. They used unmanned balloons filled with explosives.

Today, UAVs are much more advanced. Some carry supplies or weapons. Others have cameras or sensors. In 2019, UAVs were used in the Bahamas. They surveyed the damage after Hurricane Dorian hit.

DUKE

# How Drones Are Used

There are many uses for UAVs. Farmers use them to view their crops. They are also used to study weather systems. UAVs can be used for **land surveying** and filming movies too!

UAVs play an important role in search and rescue missions. They are able to cover a lot of ground in a short time. They can reach areas that are hard or dangerous for humans to reach.

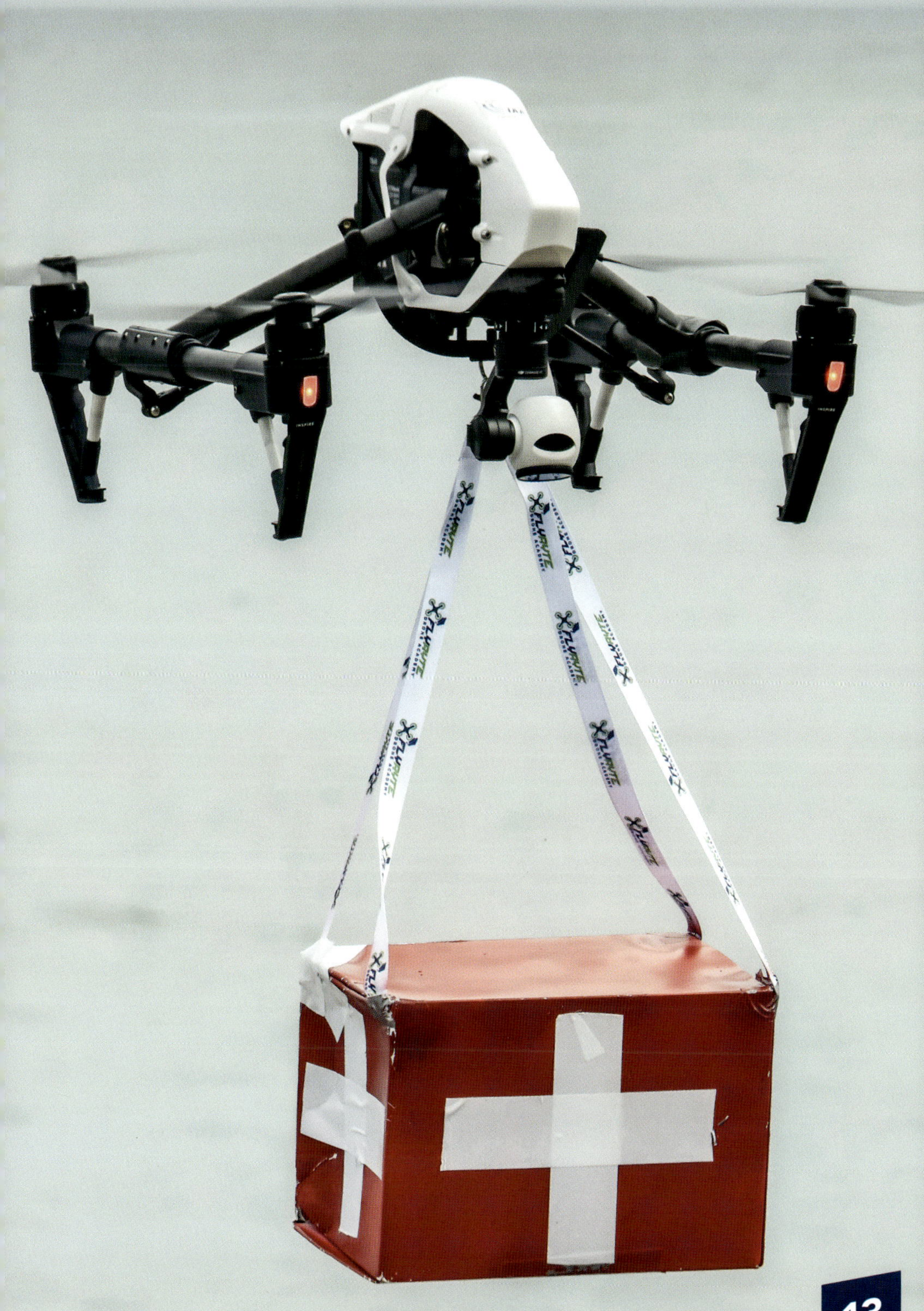

Many people use small drones for fun. Some even set up obstacle courses and race their drones! Drones are also used in sports. Some NFL teams use them at practices. They are able to get a birds-eye view of players.

# Military Drones

UAVs are used by the military too. They are mainly used for surveillance. A pilot on the ground flies the drone using radio control. The drones can mark enemy positions or survey the land. They can also take photos.

PILOT LT COL JON GREENE
SO SMSGT STEVE HENDERSON

Some military drones are used for combat. A location is set so that the UAV flies to a specific spot. The MQ-9 Reaper is used for **precision** air strikes.

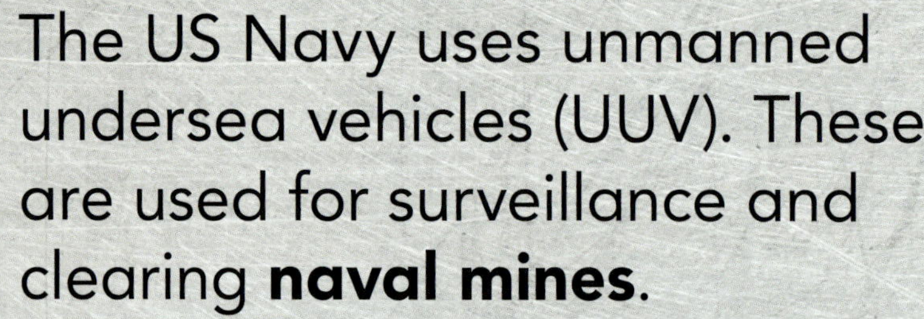

The US Navy uses unmanned undersea vehicles (UUV). These are used for surveillance and clearing **naval mines**.

Soon, they could be developed as weapons for future combat.

# More Facts

- Domino's Pizza was the first to deliver a pizza using a drone. On November 16, 2016, a drone delivered a pizza in New Zealand.

- In 2018, hundreds of drones were used in the halftime show at Super Bowl LII. Their lights formed an American flag in the sky.

- In 2019, Amazon announced that drones will soon be able to deliver some packages. They believe that many of their packages could be handled by drones.

# Glossary

**computer** – an electronic device that is used to store and sort information and work with data at a high speed.

**naval mine** – a self-contained explosive device placed in water to damage or destroy surface ships or submarines.

**land surveying** – the science and technique of accurately determining the boundaries and features of land.

**precision** – the state of being accurate or exact.

# Index



# Online Resources

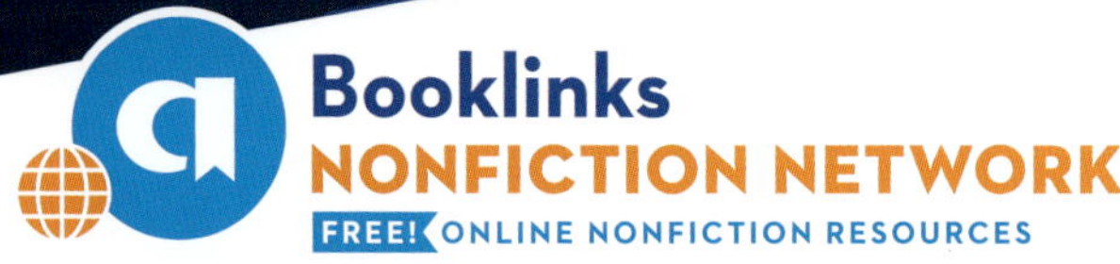


To learn more about drones, please visit **abdobooklinks.com** or scan this QR code. These links are routinely monitored and updated to provide the most current information available.